Quick-n-Easy

Natural Recipes

*These recipes use only a handful of ingredients
and take just minutes to prepare!*

D0369498

by
Lorrie Knutsen

TEACH Services, Inc.

Brushton, New York

Copyright © 1993, 1998, 2004 by Lorrie L. Knutsen
and TEACH Services, Inc.

ISBN 1-57258-275-8
Library of Congress Catalog Card Number 93-60955

Published by

TEACH Services, Inc.
254 Donovan Road
Brushton, New York 12916

Table of Contents

E-Vegetables

F-Soups

G-Desserts

H-Sandwiches

A-Breads
Breads

BASIC WHOLE WHEAT BREAD

1 c. warm water	*1 t. salt*
1 T. sweetener	
1 T. yeast	*3 c. whole wheat flour*

Dissolve sweetener in water, then stir in yeast. Let stand until yeast begins to bubble, 5 to 8 min. Add 1-1/2 c. flour and salt. Beat vigorously for 1 min. Add remaining flour gradually. Use only enough to make the dough no longer sticky. Lightly flour table and knead dough 5 min. Add more flour as necessary. Place dough in large bowl, cover with clean towel. Let dough rise until double, 30 to 45 min. Punch down, knead briefly. Squeeze out all air bubbles. Shape into loaf. Place in prepared baking pan. Cover with towel. Let rise until double in size, 30 to 45 min. Bake at 350° F. for 40 to 50 minutes, until golden brown and bread slips from the pan. Cool on a rack. *Yields:* *1 loaf.*

CRESCENTS

Divide **BASIC WHOLE WHEAT BREAD** dough in half and roll into two large circles, about 1/4 in. thick. Cut each circle into 8 wedges. Starting with wide end, roll wedge toward point. Place point side down on PAM-sprayed cookie sheet. Curve ends to form crescent. Bake 20 min. at 350° F. *Yields:* *16 crescent rolls.*

COBBLER BISCUITS

Use **BASIC WHOLE WHEAT BREAD** recipe. Prepare to pan stage. Roll out 1 in. thick and cut in circles. Place biscuits over hot thickened fruit in a casserole, then let rise for 25 to 30 min. Bake at 350° F. for 35 to 45 minutes. When done remove from oven and push biscuits down into fruit juice so they remain soft. *Yields:* *1 casserole-size cobbler.*

SESAME SEED BUNS

Use **BASIC WHOLE WHEAT BREAD** recipe. Form into buns and roll in sesame seeds. Place in muffin tins. Let rise for 25 to 30 min. Bake at 350° F. for 35 to 45 minutes. *Yields:* *18 buns.*

RASPBERRY CANES

*1 loaf **BASIC WHOLE WHEAT BREAD** dough*
2 c. bright orange dried apricots
1 (1-1/2 c.) container frozen red raspberries or frozen strawberries

Roll dough into rectangle 8" wide by 16" long. Blend 1 c. apricots and half of berries. Repeat with second half. Spread fruit mixture down the center of the rectangle lengthwise. Cut sides in half-inch strips and fold over fruit mixture to form braid. Curve end of braid to form cane. Let rise. Bake at 350° F. for 30 minutes or until golden brown. Cool. Wrap in clear cellophane and add a bow. Give! *Yields: 1 Raspberry Cane.*

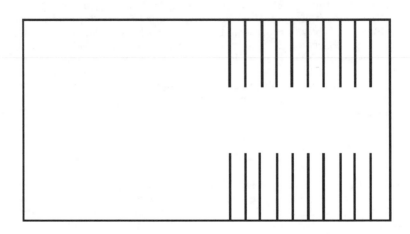

WHOLE WHEAT BURGER BUNS

3 c. warm water   *1 T. salt*
2 T. sweetener   *8–9 c. whole wheat flour*
1-1/2 T. yeast

Follow mixing directions for **BASIC WHOLE WHEAT BREAD**. Divide dough into 18–20 pieces. Shape into balls then slightly flatten by pressing between palms. Place on prepared cookie sheets, not quite touching. Let rise 20 minutes or until almost double in size. Bake at 350° F. for 25–35 minutes, until golden brown. For lighter bread or buns replace 3 c. of whole wheat flour with 3 c. of unbleached flour. *Yields: 18–20 burger buns, or 3 one-pound loaves, or 2 large loaves.*

6

WHOLE GRAIN GEMS

1 c. water   *1 t. salt*   *2-1/2 c. whole grain flour*

Combine ingredients and mix thoroughly. Knead a moment to form a soft dough. Pinch off walnut size portions and roll into balls. Place on cookie sheet. Bake at 350° F. for 15 to 25 minutes until lightly browned and baked to the center. Serve with fruit. *Yields: 2 dozen gems.*

SESAME TOAST

6 Slices whole-grain bread   *1/2 c. sesame seeds*

Place two dinner plates on a level counter. Into one pour water to a depth of about 1/8 inch; in the other spread sesame seeds to about 1/4 inch depth. Press one side of each slice of bread into water. Press moistened surface of slice into sesame seeds. The seeds will stick to the moistened bread. Place bread, sesame seed side up, on a cookie sheet. Toast under broiler until golden and crispy. Watch carefully as seeds tend to burn quickly. May be enjoyed warm or cold. *Yields: 6 toasts.*

PITA (POCKET BREAD)

3–4 c. whole wheat pastry flour
or a mixture of whole wheat flour and unbleached wheat flour
1/2 t. salt   *1 T. yeast (1 pkg.)*
2 c. water, very warm   *1 T. honey*

Dissolve yeast and honey in water and allow yeast five minutes to soften. Add flour and salt. Knead until smooth, adding flour if needed. Cut into 24 balls; knead each ball until very smooth and round. Cover and let rise about an hour. Flatten out balls with a rolling pin on a floured surface. Place on a cookie sheet and let rise about 45 minutes or more until slightly puffed. Being extremely careful to touch only the very edge, gently and quickly slip the flat breads from the cookie sheet to a griddle or other baking sheet that has been heated to oven temperature. This sudden change of temperature seals the pocked bread on the outside and begins to expand the moisture inside, causing the bread to form a "balloon" or pocket. Bake in very hot oven, 550° F. or as hot as oven will go, for about two minutes or until lightly browned and puffed in center. Be very careful to remove the pocket breads before they become crisp shells. Cool on rack and store in plastic bag until ready for use. Cut pocket breads in half crosswise and fill with any sandwich mixture: beans, sprouts, lentils, tossed salads, etc. *Yields: 24 Pitas.*

SAVORY BREADCRUMBS

1 c. breadcrumbs	*1/2 t. paprika*
1/4 c. ground walnuts	*Pinch of salt*
1/4 t. onion powder	

Mix all ingredients. May be used as a topping for casseroles. Or double the recipe and use as a breading mixture. ***Yields:*** *1 c. breadcrumbs.*

DIASTATIC MALT

Barley or other grain soaked in water and spread thinly on a shallow pan or cookie sheet until it sprouts, then dried and aged, has a sweet taste. This simple whole-grain sweetener is called diastatic malt.

Diastatic malt, which is widely used in Europe, can be used in any bread recipe to replace the sugar used to feed the yeast. It will make the crust brown and improve the flavor. Diabetics and hypoglycemics especially will appreciate this inexpensive natural sweetener.

1 to 2 cups whole wheat
3 c. lukewarm water

Place the wheat in the water in a quart jar for 24 hours. Drain well and pour the wheat into a plastic sprouter or leave in jar, turning the jar on its side. Cover with a cloth. Rinse and drain at least twice daily until the sprout is slightly longer than the seed. This takes about 48 hours. Place sprouted wheat on a large baking sheet and bake at 150° F. until thoroughly dry, about 3 to 4 hours. Or dry in a food dehydrator. Place the dry sprouted wheat in a blender and blend on high for about 30 to 45 seconds or until it is a fine meal consistency. Store diastatic malt in a tightly closed glass jar in the refrigerator or freezer. It will keep indefinitely. Use in any bread recipe; eliminate or reduce the amount of sweetener in the bread. Use 1 t. diastatic malt for each 2 loaves of bread or each five cups of flour. Use on cereal as a natural sweetener if desired.

Crackers

SESAME OAT CRACKERS

1 c. water	*1/4 t. salt*
1 c. rolled oats	*Sesame seeds*

Blend water, oats, sunflower seeds and salt 45–60 seconds, until smooth. Pour immediately onto a non-stick 11" x 16" edged baking sheet. Sprinkle generously with sesame seeds. Bake 10 minutes at 325° F. Remove from oven and score by pressing knife into dough. Return to oven for 30 minutes or until crisp, dry, and golden brown. If the batter is not evenly distributed on the pan, the outer edge crackers may be thinner and may finish baking before those in the center of the pan. Simply remove the finished crackers and return the remaining crackers to the oven for longer baking. Store crackers in an air-tight container. ***Yields:*** *2 to 3 dozen crackers.*

SUNFLOWER AND OAT CRACKERS

3 c. oats	*3/4 c. sunflower seeds*
1-1/4 c. water	*1-1/2 t. salt*

Blend seeds in 1/2 c. water until smooth. Combine remaining ingredients and kneed well for a smooth dough, about 5 minutes. Roll into thin log and slice into 1 inch pieces. Flatten each piece with a dough press or rolling pin. Make them very thin. This can be done by rolling them between two sheets of plastic bag, then removing one sheet and placing the crackers on a baking sheet, then peel off the second layer of plastic. Bake about 10 minutes at 350° F. or until crisp. Watch closely as these crackers will burn. ***Yields:*** *2 to 3 dozen crackers*

EASY CORN CHIPS

Corn tortillas made of only corn and water
Salt

Dip each tortilla into salt water and lay on a paper towel to absorb excess water. With a sharp knife cut each tortilla into six wedges. Arrange tortilla wedges on a non stick cookie sheet and heat to dry in oven. At 350° F. it takes 10 to 20 minutes. Watch closely to prevent burning.

Note: Read ingredient list on purchased tortillas to assure a simple, wholesome product.

Muffins

SIMPLE CORN MUFFINS

1/4 c. shredded coconut, opt.
1-1/2 c. corn meal
1/4 c. whole wheat flour

1/3 c. water
1 t. salt, scant

Mix all ingredients. Let stand 20 to 30 minutes before shaping muffins. Bake 45 minutes at 350° F. *Yields:* 6 small muffins.

APPLESAUCE MUFFINS

2 to 3 c. applesauce
1-1/2 c. rye flakes
1-1/2 c. rolled barley

3 c. chopped dates
1 c. orange juice concentrate

Combine all ingredients and let stand for a few minutes to allow absorption of moisture. Place papers in muffin tins or spray with PAM and coat with bran. Fill, rounding tops. Bake at 350° F. for 25 minutes or until lightly browned. *Yields:* 16 muffins.

APPLE-OATMEAL MUFFINS

1/2 c. raisins or
    chopped dates
1 c. finely shredded apples

1-1/2 c. rolled oats
1/2 c. chopped nuts, fine
1/2 t. salt

Soften dates in small amount of water and mash. Combine all ingredients. Let stand until moisture is absorbed. Mix together lightly with fingers or fork. With spoon, pack lightly into muffin pans. Fill well and round nicely. Bake at 375° for 25 minutes or longer. *Yields:* 12 muffins.

FRESH FRUIT MUFFINS

1/2–3/4 c. chopped dates
    or other dried fruit
2 c. rolled oats

2 c. w.w. flour
1/2 t. salt
3 c. crushed fruit
    (pulp and juice)

Stir all together. May need more flour or liquid, depending on how juicy your fruit is. Thaw frozen fruit before using. Put in muffin tins; bake at 350° F. for 50 minutes or until firm to the touch. *Yields:* 24 muffins.

Recipes in **BOLD PRINT** *are listed in the index.*

DATE MUFFINS

2 T. yeast
1/2 c. lukewarm water
1-1/2 c. chopped dates
2 t. salt

2 c. hot water
3-1/2 c. w.w. flour
2 c. oatmeal

Soften yeast in lukewarm water. Set aside. In separate bowl, mix together dates, salt and hot water. Add flour and oatmeal. When cool enough add yeast. Stir well. Fill muffin cups one-half full. Let rise until double. Bake at 350° F. for about 20 to 30 minutes. (You may have to add 1/2 c. more water to get right consistency.) Reheat before serving. *Yields: 16 muffins.*

ENGLISH MUFFINS

1 c. warm water
1 T. yeast
2 t. honey

1 t. salt
3 c. whole wheat flour

Soften yeast in warm water. Stir in other ingredients. Mix well until dough is soft. Roll out on cornmeal-covered surface to 1/4 inch thick. Cut into 4 inch circles. Place on baking sheet. Let rise until doubled. Bake at 350° F. for 5 minutes. Turn muffins over and bake for another 7 minutes. *Yields: 16 to 18 English muffins.*

Kuchens

KUCHEN

1/4 of 1 loaf **BASIC WHOLE WHEAT BREAD** dough
1/2 c. water
3 pitted dates

1/2 T. arrowroot powder
   or corn starch
2 c. assorted fresh, canned,
   or dried fruit pieces

Roll yeast dough to 1/4 inch thickness and fit onto a pizza pan or pie plate. Blend water, dates, and arrowroot powder or corn starch until very smooth. Pour over dough and smooth to edges. Top with fruit pieces arranged over the surface. Bake at 350° F. for 25 to 35 minutes or until crust is nicely browned and filling is set. Cool and refrigerate or freeze. Reheat in a microwave (or regular oven in a covered container or in foil) and serve hot. *Yields: 1 Kuchen.*

B-Breakfasts
Waffles

OAT WAFFLES

2 c. water   2 c. oats   1/2 t. salt

Blend until smooth. Pour 1-cupful of batter onto hot waffle iron. Bake 10–20 minutes, depending upon the heat of the waffle iron. Waffles will be crisp, light and dry when finished. Can be made a day ahead and refrigerated or can be packaged in plastic bags and frozen, then thawed in an oven, microwave or toaster. **Yields:** *2 to 3 waffles.*

RICE WAFFLES

2 c. water   2 c. rolled oats
1 c. rice flour   1/4 to 1/2 t. salt
1-1/2 c. water

Blend first three ingredients together until smooth. Add rice flour and additional water. Pour batter into the center of a hot, seasoned waffle iron until it spreads to the edges and remain slightly higher in the center. Close waffle iron; bake 10 minutes, or the time needed with your particular waffle iron. Don't peek! **Yields:** *3 to 4 waffles.*
[Add more water to adjust batter to your desired thinness; thinner batter makes lighter waffles. Experiment.]

APPLE PIE WAFFLE

3/4 c. coconut   1 t. vanilla
4 T. corn starch   1/2 c. grated apple
    or arrowroot powder   2 to 3 c. water

Combine all ingredients except the grated apple and blend until creamy and smooth, adding water to make a thick but pourable batter. Fold in grated apple. Preheat waffle iron and prepare with a brushing of Tahini or a spray of Pam if needed. Bake waffle 10 minutes. **Yields**: *2 waffles.*

Recipes in **BOLD PRINT** *are listed in the index.*

Toasts

PINEAPPLE-APRICOT FRUIT TOAST

1 can apricot halves
1 can pineapple tidbits

8 slices whole-grain toast

1 can apricot nectar
4 T. arrowroot powder
or cornstarch

Drain fruit and combine the juices in a saucepan with arrowroot powder or cornstarch. Stir over medium heat until thickened and clear. Add fruit pieces and mix well. Spoon over toast and serve hot for breakfast. *Yields: 4 servings.*

MIXED FRUIT OVER TOAST

1 can peaches,
cut in 1/2 inch pieces
1 can pineapple tidbits

8 slices whole-grain toast

1 can pears,
cut in 1/2 inch pieces
4 T. arrowroot powder
or cornstarch

Drain all fruit and combine the juice in a saucepan with arrowroot powder or cornstarch. Stir over medium heat until thickened and clear. Add fruit pieces and mix well. Spoon over toast and serve hot for breakfast. *Yields: 4 servings.*

APPLESAUCE OVER TOAST

4 c. applesauce, unsweetened
or home canned if possible

8 slices whole-grain toast

1/2 c. unsweetened coconut,
shredded fine

Heat applesauce in saucepan or microwave oven. Spread over toast and, if desired, sprinkle with coconut. Serve immediately. *Yields: 8 serving.*

OATMEAL FRENCH TOAST

1 c. quick rolled oats
1/3 c. sesame seeds
1-3/4 c. water

1 t. salt
2 T. sweetener

8 slices whole-grain bread

Blend all ingredients until smooth. Let stand 3 minutes to absorb moisture. Dip slices of bread in batter and place on non-stick cookie sheets. Bake 25 minutes at 350° F. Serve hot with fruit sauce or fruit jam. *Yields: 4 servings.*

BANANA FRENCH TOAST

3/4 c. water
2 dates
1/2 c. cashews

3 bananas
6 slices whole grain toast

Whiz nuts, water and dates in blender. Add bananas and whiz again. Dip toast in mixture and place on floured or Pam-sprayed baking sheet. Broil until golden. Turn and broil other side. Top with applesauce or strawberries and serve. *Yields: 6 servings.*

APPLESAUCE TREATS

8 slices whole-grain bread
4 c. applesauce, unsweetened
   or home canned if possible
1/2 c. unsweetened coconut, shredded fine
   or chopped nuts

Spread applesauce over bread and sprinkle with coconut or chopped nuts. Place on cookie sheets. Bake at 350° F. for 20 minutes. Serve immediately. *Yields: 4 servings.*

14

Hot Cereals

COOKING SIMPLE BROWN RICE

1 c. raw brown rice
4 c. water   1 t. salt

Bring water and salt to boil in a covered saucepan. Stir in grain. Cover and return to boil. Turn heat down to simmer and cook for recommended length of time, about 60 minutes. For the fluffiest rice, do not stir the grain after mixing with boiling water. *Yields: 4 c. cooked rice.*

ORANGE-BANANA SAUCE OVER BROWN RICE

4 c. cooked brown rice   1 recipe **ORANGE-BANANA SAUCE**

Spread 1 cup brown rice on each plate. Pour **ORANGE-BANANA SAUCE** over rice. Garnish with a sprinkle of coconut, slivered almonds, or granola if desired. Add chopped dates or other dried fruit pieces if desired. *Yields: 4 servings.*

CORN MEAL MUSH

1 c. corn meal   3/4 c. cold water
2-1/2 c. boiling water   1/2 t. salt

Blend the corn meal with the cold water, pour into the salted boiling water and stir until it boils again. Let corn meal boil quite rapidly until it begins to thicken. Reduce heat to low and simmer for 20–40 minutes. Serve topped with applesauce. *Yields: 4 servings.*

WHOLE MILLET CEREAL

1 c. millet   1 t. salt   5 c. water

Combine. Bring to boil, cover and simmer 45–60 minutes, until water is absorbed. *Yields: Six 2/3-cup servings.*

MILLET BREAKFAST DISH

1/2 c. cornmeal
1/2 c. millet
3 c. water

1/2 t. salt
1/2 c. chopped dates

Simmer millet and cornmeal in salted water for about 1 hour. Add dates and serve hot. *Yields: 4 servings.*

HOT CRACKED WHEAT CEREAL

1/2 c. cracked wheat
2 c. water
8 chopped pitted dates

3 T. coconut
unsweetened
1/2 t. salt

Dextrinize cracked wheat by stirring constantly in dry pan over low heat for several minutes or until lightly browned. Then add remaining ingredients. Bring to boil and simmer 15–20 minutes. Each cup serving contains 10 grams of protein. *Yields: 2–3 servings.*

FRUIT-FILLED OATS

4 c. boiling water
1 t. salt
1-3/4 c. oats

1/4 c. dates or other dried fruit
1 large banana, chopped

Mix ingredients in the order given except for the banana. Heat in saucepan on medium heat. Reduce heat and simmer 45–60 minutes. Stir in banana just before serving. *Yields: 4 servings.*

GRAPENUTS OATMEAL

3/4 c. soy or thin nut milk
1/3 c. dry quick oats
1/3 c. Grapenuts cereal

1 to 2 t. honey or
2 T. chopped dried fruit
(dates, raisins, etc.)

Place milk and oats in a saucepan, bring to a boil and remove from heat. Add Grapenuts and your choice of sweetener. Cover; let set for just a few minutes. *Yields: 1 serving.*

Cold Cereals

BREAKFAST BANANA SPLIT

Millet, rice or oats, cooked
Bananas

Strawberries, partially mashed
Blueberries, partially mashed
Carob Sauce

Use ice cream scoop to make three scoops of cooked cereal in a row. Split peeled banana and place half on each side of cereal. Top one scoop of cereal with strawberries, the center scoop with carob sauce, and the third with blueberries. (For fresh berries, slice or put on whole. If using canned or frozen berries, pour off juice into a saucepan and thicken with 1 T. arrowroot powder or corn starch stirred into juice before heating. Heat to boiling, stirring constantly. Add fruit.) Sprinkle with chopped nuts or coconut.

CAROB SAUCE

2 c. water
1/3 c. pure maple syrup
  or 1/2 c. chopped dates
1 t. vanilla, optional

1/2 c. carob powder
2 T. arrowroot powder
  or corn starch

Liquify all ingredients in blender. Cook over medium heat until thickened, stirring constantly.

CASHEW "WHIPPED CREAM"

3/4 c. cashews or blanched almonds
1-1/2 c. cooked millet
1 t. pure vanilla

1/2 c. water
1/4 c. pure maple syrup

Whiz nuts in blender until very fine. Add remaining ingredients and blend until very creamy. Amount of water needed will vary depending upon the moistness of the grain. Other cooked grains may be used instead of millet. Buckwheat works well. Barley and oats tend to be "gooey." Cashews and millet seem to give the most creamy texture. Chill well.

SIMPLE GRANOLA

2 c. rolled oats
1 c. shredded coconut, unsweetened
1 c. water
1 apple, medium to large, any kind
1/2 c. dried fruit (dates, apricots, apples, etc.), optional

In a large mixing bowl combine oats and coconut. In a blender whiz apple (quartered and cored) in water. Pour liquid over dry ingredients and toss until all is moistened. Spread loosely on a 12" x 15" cookie sheet and bake at 250°F. for 6 to 10 hours, until golden brown and thoroughly dry. (Occasional stirring may be necessary if the granola is not drying evenly.) Add the dried fruit after the granola is baked and cooled. Store in a dry place for use as a breakfast cereal, a topping over fruit, or just as a light snack with any meal. Serve with fruit sauce, fruit juice, or sliced fruit. Also makes a nice garnish over fruit salads, in fruit soups, etc. *Yields: 3 cups without dried fruit; 3-1/2 cups with fruit.*

Breakfast Entrées

FRUIT BETTY

4 c. thickened fruit
3 slices whole grain bread,
    crumbled

2 T. date butter
2 T. chopped nuts or
    coconut

Mix crumbled bread with date butter and nuts. Put favorite thickened fruit in baking dish. Top with bread mixture. Bake at 325° F. for 20–30 minutes. Makes a nice dessert or breakfast. *Yields: 4 servings.*

SCALLOPED APPLES

2 c. soft bread crumbs
1/4 c. nuts, chopped fine
3 c. apples, chopped

1/2 c. dates
1/2 c. water

Simmer dates in water until soft. Mix with other ingredients. Put in baking dish. Bake for 30 minutes at 350° F. *Yields: 6 servings.*

18

BAKED APPLES

4 cooking apples
3/4 c. orange juice
2 T. chopped nuts

3 T. date butter
4 T. bread or cracker crumbs

Wash and core apples. [May slice in half if desired.] Make filling of remaining ingredients mixed together and pack in each apple. Place in casserole dish. Bake 25 minutes at 425° F. *Yields: 4 servings.*

RASPBERRY AUF LAUF

4 c. applesauce
3 c. raspberries, fresh or frozen

4 c. whole wheat bread cubes
3/4 c. coconut, if desired

Mix first three ingredients together and pour into an oblong baking dish. Sprinkle coconut on top, if desired. Bake 25 minutes at 350° F. Or mix the night before, refrigerate, and heat for breakfast the next morning. *Yields: 6 servings.*

RICE BREAKFAST PATTIES

3 T. flour
2 T. date butter

2 c. cooked rice, unsalted, well done
1/4 to 1/2 c. water

Mix all ingredients. Mixture should be stiff. Add only enough water and flour so you can make patties. Form into 1/4 c. patties. Bake in a 350° oven 45–60 minutes or to a golden brown. *Yields: 8 patties.*

GRANOLA PUDDING

Layer 3 c. granola with 3 c. applesauce. Set overnight in covered baking dish in refrigerator. Heat 20 minutes at 350° F. *Yields: 6 servings.*

LENTIL PORRIDGE

1 c. lentils, uncooked
1/2 c. hulled millet
5 c. water

1 bay leaf
2 t. onion powder
1-1/4 t. salt

Bring to boil. Simmer 1 hour. Remove bay leaf. Serve with melons for breakfast. *Yields: 4 servings.*

Fresh Fruit Ideas

MELON BALL RAINBOW

Using the melon ball maker, prepare the balls from cantaloupe, Crenshaw, Persian melon, casaba, watermelon, etc. Serve one kind or a combination in any fruit juice. Always have melon balls and juice chilled. Garnish simply with a mint sprig.

AMBROSIA

3 large oranges
2 ripe bananas, sliced

3 T. fresh grated orange rind
1/2 c. coconut, unsweetened, grated

Peel, quarter, and remove seeds from oranges. Blend in blender until fine. Mix all ingredients. Garnish with mint sprigs or sweet basil. **Yields:** *5 to 6 servings.*

GRAPEFRUIT BOATS

Slice grapefruit in half. Carefully remove the sections and set aside. Scoop out all the inner peeling and dividers. Fill grapefruit half with grapefruit segments, mandarin oranges, pineapple tidbits, oranges or kiwi.

FRESH FRUIT PLATE

Select fresh, ripe fruit which is in season. Cut into attractive shapes and arrange nicely on platter or large plate. May accompany a meal as the dessert or be used with breads and crackers to make a complete meal.

ORANGE "SMILIES"

Select fresh, ripe oranges in season. Cut each orange into eight wedges cross-wise and arrange on platter. May place kiwi, pineapple, or strawberry slices between orange "smilies" for added color.

Recipes in **BOLD PRINT** *are listed in the index.*

Fruit Syrups and Sauces

PEACH SAUCE

Blend peaches and juice or syrup together for a delicious sauce. Use home-canned peaches for best flavor. Otherwise use peaches canned in their own juice or in other fruit juices. These are available in most grocery stores now. Try other fruits. Pears are good, too.

DRIED FRUIT SAUCE

1/3 c. dates	1/3 c. dried apples
1/3 c. dried peaches	3 c. HOT pineapple juice

Soak all ingredients together for 1/2 hour. Blend together in blender, adding a bit more juice if needed.

FRUIT SYRUP

12 oz. can unsweetened juice concentrate (your choice)	1 c. water
	2 T. arrowroot powder or cornstarch

Combine ingredients in saucepan and heat over medium heat, stirring constantly, until thickened. Can add finely chopped, canned, dried or fresh fruit if desired.

PEACH-PEAR SAUCE

2 c. canned peaches	2 c. canned pears
5 dates	2 T. arrowroot powder or cornstarch

Drain fruit and save juice. Blend 1/2 c. each of peaches and pears with juice and dates. Heat over stove and thicken with arrowroot powder or cornstarch mixed with 2 T. cold water. Cut remaining fruit into 1/2 inch pieces and add to juice mixture.

BLUEBERRY SAUCE

1 quart sweet grape juice
2 to 4 T. arrowroot powder or corn starch
1/4 c. honey [optional, depending on flavor of juice]
2 c. frozen blueberries

Heat juice, arrowroot powder or corn starch and honey until thickened. Stir in blueberries and serve over toast or waffles. Can place mixture in baking dish and cover with granola for a crisp.

ORANGE-BANANA SAUCE

2 bananas, fresh or frozen   *1 c. orange juice*

Blend together. Use as a sauce over pancakes, waffles, toast, cooked rice or other cooked cereals.

FRESH APPLESAUCE

6–8 apples   *1 c. water*

Quarter and core apples. Cut into small pieces. Start with 1/2 c. water in blender and 1 c. apple pieces. Blend together. Add more apples pieces at the blender purees each addition. Add only enough more water to enable the blender to continue moving sauce. Serve immediately over granola, toast, french toast, waffles or pancakes. *Yields: Four 1/2-cup servings.*

Fresh fruits and vegetables are *live foods.* Any food which has been cooked, canned, or frozen is no longer alive. The enzymes present in all whole, fresh food have been destroyed and the food construction changed. Your health will greatly improve with the increased use of live foods rather than dead ones. Whole grains, which have dried into a storage form, are nutritious, but not fresh. They are not usable to the body uncooked, and must therefore be cooked well—until soft and palatable.

RASPBERRY-APPLESAUCE

4 c. fresh or canned applesauce   *1 c. fresh or frozen raspberries*

Heat applesauce. Add raspberries and stir just enough to evenly mix through the sauce. Stirring will juice the berries and turn sauce red.

Non-Dairy Milk Ideas

RICE MILK

1 c. cooked brown rice or millet
3–4 c. water　　　　　　　*1/4 t. vanilla*
1/8 t. salt　　　　　　　　*1 T. honey, optional*

Blend rice and 1 c. water until creamy. Add enough water to make a quart of milk or to make milk the desired consistency. Season to taste. Experiment to find a texture, color, and flavor your family enjoys. ***Yields:*** *4 to 5 cups rice milk.*

ALMOND MILK

3/4 c. raw, whole almonds　　*1/8 t. salt*
12 dates or 2 T. honey　　　　*2 c. hot water*
2 t. vanilla　　　　　　　　　*4 c. cold water*

Blend first 5 ingredients. Add remaining water, stir and chill. ***Yields:*** *6 cups almond milk.*

PEAR MILK

1/3 to 1/2 c. almonds or cashews
1 c. water　　　　　　　　*1 can canned pears*
1/4 t. vanilla　　　　　　　*Juice from pears*
1/8 t. salt　　　　　　　　*1 T. honey, optional*

Blend all ingredients except pears till creamy. Add enough canned pears (depending on how thick you want it) and juice to make a quart of milk. ***Yields:*** *4 cups pear milk.*

BABY'S MILKSHAKES

Blend cooked whole grains and fresh or canned fruits in soy milk to make delightful milkshakes for infants and toddlers. Proportions and choices of grains and fruits are entirely your choice.

SOY MILK

1 c. soaked soy beans (1\3 c. dry beans)
2 c. warm water   2 T. honey
2 c. boiling water   1/2 t. salt

1 strainer   1 piece of strainer cloth or cheesecloth
                    (a clean man's white handkerchief will suffice)

Soak beans in water for 6 hours or overnight. Place 1 c. soaked soybeans and 2 c. of water in blender. Liquefy. Strain bean mixture through a clean strainer cloth or cheesecloth. Wring the pulp until it is almost dry. Add 2 c. boiling water to the bean "milk" and boil over low heat for 30 minutes or cook in a double boiler. Add honey and salt to taste. Pour into a glass jar or bottle, cover tightly and place in refrigerator. This soy milk remains fresh for several days if kept refrigerated at 30° to 40° F. Save the pulp for use in patties, casseroles and similar main dishes, waffles and breads. *Yields:* *4 c. soy milk.*

Soy milk properly made is a wonderful food for the sick. Soy milk does not form curds in the stomach and putrefy as cows or goat's milk does, and can be used in the same ways as they are used. The beauty of it is that soy milk is highly alkaline and well adapted to the needs of the human system, for both adults and children. The following chart, provided by the Unites States Department of Agriculture, Bureau of Chemistry and Soils, Washington, D.C., compares several kinds of milk:

Milk	Water	Ash	Prot.	Fat	Carb.
Human	89.95%	0.25%	1.30%	2.50%	6.00%
Cow	87.30%	0.80%	3.20%	3.50%	5.20%
Goat	87.00%	0.50%	4.00%	4.50%	4.00%
Soybean	87.03%	0.52%	2.40%	3.15%	6.90%
Nut	87.00%	2.03%	5.60%	5.50%	7.23%

C-Entrees
Rice and Pasta Dishes

BROWN RICE DELIGHT

4 c. hot cooked brown rice
1 ripe avocado

1 can pitted black olives
2 c. tomato puree, seasoned to taste
1–2 ripe tomatoes, chopped

Place 1 c. rice on each plate. Top with tomato puree, chopped or whole olives, avocado, and tomatoes. ***Yields:*** *4 servings.*

BAKED BROWN RICE *"FLUFFY EVERY TIME."*

1 c. brown rice
2-1/2 c. boiling water

1/2 t. salt

Toast rice in cast iron skillet over medium heat stirring frequently until rice is a light golden brown. Bring water to a boil. Transfer rice to 1 quart casserole dish. Stir in water and salt. Bake covered at 350 ° for 45 minutes. ***Yields:*** *3 cups.*
Variations: Use seasoned broth instead of water and add chopped onions.

GARBANZO-RICE LOAF

1-1/2 c. garbanzos, cooked
3/4 c. water

1-1/2 c. brown rice, cooked

1/2 t. onion salt
1/4 t. garlic powder

Blend garbanzos with water until smooth. Combine remaining ingredients. Mix well. Pour into casserole. Bake 45 minutes at 350° F. Pleasant texture added by 1/2 c. slivered almonds mixed into casserole or used as a garnish after baking. ***Yields:*** *4 to 6 servings.*

WHOLE WHEAT SPAGHETTI
WITH BROCCOLI SAUCE

4 to 8 oz. sliced eggplant
1 pound broccoli spears, thinly sliced
3 stalks of celery, thinly sliced
4 green onions, cut fine
2 heaping T. arrowroot
   or corn starch in 1/4 c. cold water

Cook 8 oz. whole wheat spaghetti. While spaghetti is boiling in salted water, prepare the sauce. Saute broccoli, celery, onions in 1/4 c. water. Add eggplant. Drain the spaghetti and reserve the cooking liquid. Mix arrowroot or cornstarch and two cups of the spaghetti water. Pour immediately over the vegetables and heat and stir until sauce is thick. Season with salt and herbs to taste. Serve spaghetti on a large platter with the sauce poured over and garnished with lightly toasted sunflower seeds. **Yields:** *4 to 6 servings.*

BAKED MACARONI AND LENTILS

3/4 c. lentils
2 c. w. w. macaroni
1 big onion, chopped

1/2 c. tomato sauce
1/2 green pepper,
   chopped

Cover lentils 1/2 inch with water and cook 1–2 hours. Cook macaroni in 3 c. water. Drain. Add lentils to the macaroni. Saute onion and green pepper in a little water until soft; mix with macaroni and lentils. Pour into floured baking dish. Cover with fine bread crumbs if desired. Bake at 350° F. for 25 minutes. **Yields:** *4 servings.*

ORIENTAL SPAGHETTI

16 oz. cooked spaghetti
16 oz. frozen oriental vegetables or similar fresh, cut, mixed vegetables
Slivered almonds
Bragg's Aminos to taste [a Soy Sauce substitute]*

Cook spaghetti and set aside. Steam vegetables with almonds. Brown sesame seeds in a non-stick skillet. Stir all together. Serve immediately. **Yields:** *6 servings.*

*Bragg's Aminos, an unfermented soy sauce, is available in the seasoning section of most stores.

*Recipes in **BOLD PRINT** are listed in the index.*

Loafs

TOMATO-MILLET LOAF
OR COLD CUTS

4-1/4 c. tomato juice or blenderized tomatoes
1 medium onion, chopped or 2 t. onion powder
1/2 c. raw sunflower seed, sesame seed or cashews
1/2 c. chopped olives or chopped nuts
1 c. uncooked millet

Blend onion and sunflower seeds in 1 c. of tomato juice. When very smooth, add remaining tomato juice and combine with olives and millet in a non-stick or heavy sauce pan. Cover, bring to a boil, then turn heat very low and simmer 45 minutes to 1 hour. Serve in a pretty casserole dish, garnished with a few green onion stems cut into tiny rings. Or chill and slice for sandwich cold cuts. *Yields: 6 to 8 servings.*

PECAN LOAF

1 c. pecan (or walnut) meal
1/2 c. sunflower seeds
2 c. cooked brown rice
3 c. soft w.w. bread crumbs (large crumbs)
2 t. onion salt

Combine all ingredients. Mix well. Pack firmly into a loaf pan. Bake at 375° F. for 1/2 hour. *Yields: 6 to 8 servings.*

RICE LOAF

8 c. rice, cooked
3/4 c. uncooked cornmeal
1/4 c. pecans, ground

1 T. onion powder
1/2 t. sage

Mix all ingredients. Press into 8" x 12" cake pan. Bake at 350° F. for one hour. *Yields: 4 to 6 servings.*

Beans and Lentils

SIMPLE CROCK-POT BEANS

1 c. dry beans of your choice   1 t. salt
Water to cover beans by 3 inches

Soak beans overnight and place in crock-pot with water to cover (or place unsoaked beans in water in crock-pot), set crock-pot on high and cook for 8 hours or overnight.   Add salt at the beginning of the cooking time for best flavor.   Can use soybeans, pinto beans, kidney beans, black beans, garbanzos, navy or northern white beans, or adzuki beans. *Yields:* 4 (1/2-cup) servings.
Variations: Beans can be used in tacos, haystacks, burritos, chapatis, as a sandwich spread or with cornbread, in pita or pocket bread, over rice or just enjoyed alone.

FAVORITE LENTIL LOAF

1 medium onion   2 c. cooked lentils
2 c. mashed potatoes   1/3 c. soy flour
1/3 c. wheat germ

Steam onion in 1/4 c. water (may add 1/4 t. each savory and marjoram). Add remaining ingredients and mix well. Salt to taste or add a favorite vegetable seasoning. Bake in loaf pan 350° F. for 1 hour. Cool a few minutes and turn out of loaf pan onto serving platter. Garnish and serve. *Yields:* 4 to 6 servings.

SOY OR GARBANZO SOUFFLÉ

1-1/2 c. soaked soy   1/2 t. salt
  or garbanzo beans   1/2 c. onion, chopped
2 c. tomato juice   1/4 c. olives, chopped
  or stewed tomatoes

Blend smooth all but olives. Stir all ingredients and pour into Pam-sprayed 8" x 8" baking dish. Bake, uncovered, at 350° F. for 60 minutes. Serve hot or cold, plain or with tomato sauce, as a sandwich filling or main dish. *Yields:* 6 to 8 servings.

*Recipes in **BOLD PRINT** are listed in the index.*

BEAN TORTILLA FILLING

2 lg. cans light red kidney beans   *2 tomatoes*
2 medium onion, chopped fine   *1 can olives*

Drain liquid off into a bowl. Place 1 can of beans in blender. Blend until smooth, adding a little liquid at a time until you have added enough to get proper consistency. (The liquid in the blender should form a slight funnel toward the blades when the thickness is right.) Scoop pureed beans into a bowl and repeat with second can. Season according to your families use of herbs and seasonings. Onions (or onion powder) and garlic (or garlic powder) are good. Cut up tomato and onion and olives. Stir into beans. Spoon onto tortilla shells. Fold and place in a flat baking dish. Bake at 325° F. about 30 minutes. Serve with **GUACAMOLE** (p. 56). *Yields: 8 to 12 tacos.*

FLOUR TORTILLAS

2 c. w.w. flour
3/4 c. warm water   *1/2 t. salt*

Place flour and salt in a bowl and stir in the warm water to make a soft dough. Add flour, a little at a time, and knead until it is elastic and no longer sticky. Form into golf ball-sized balls. Dip each ball in flour, one at a time, and roll out to a 7 inch round (about 1/8 inch thick). Bake on a dry, medium hot griddle or skillet (cast iron is best). When the upper side turns color, turn over for a few second, then return to the first side and press with a cloth, using a rotating motion. Use as you would a tortilla. It takes practice to make chapatties round, but they taste good regardless of shape. *Yields: 12 taco shells.*

CARROT-BEAN CROQUETTES

1 medium onion, diced   *1/2 c. bread crumbs*
1 c. mashed pinto beans   *1/4 t. sage*
1-1/2 c. raw carrots, grated   *Pinch of salt*

Combine all ingredients and mix well. Form into balls and roll in fine bread crumbs. Bake on ungreased baking sheet for 15 to 20 minutes at 375° F. Serve with your favorite sauce. *Yields: 5 (1/2-cup) servings.*

LENTILS AND BROCCOLI

1 onion, chopped, steamed alone
1 clove garlic, minced, steamed alone
3 c. lentils, sprouted, steamed alone
1 c. broccoli, chopped, steamed alone
salt or Jensen's Natural Vegetable Seasoning to taste

Steam first four ingredients. Add seasonings and serve. ***Yields:*** *6 servings.*

Pizza

NON-CHEESE PIZZA

2 pizza shells　　　　　　　　*1 medium sized can tomato puree*
Garlic powder　　　　　　　　*Oregano*
Sweet basil　　　　　　　　　*Italian seasoning*
1 can olives　　　　　　　　　*Cut up vegetables:*
　　　　　　　　　　　　　　　　onion, green pepper, etc.

Pour tomato sauce over crusts. Spread with spatula or fork. Sprinkle seasonings over top. Then put on cut up vegetables of your choosing. Bake at 400° F. for 20–30 minutes or until done. Serve with salad. Makes a complete meal. ***Yields:*** *8 servings.*

WHOLE WHEAT PIZZA CRUST

2 c. very warm water　　　　　*1-1/2 t. salt*
2 T. active dry yeast　　　　　*5 c. w. wheat flour*
2 T. honey

Combine ingredients. Mix well; kneed well. Let rise once, 30 minutes; place on cookie sheet, pizza pan or jelly roll pan sprayed with Pam. Wet hands a little and spread into a crust by pressing out with the fingertips. ***Yields:*** *2 pizza crusts.*

Recipes in **BOLD PRINT** *are listed in the index.*

D-Salads
Vegetable Salads

POTATO SALAD

8 medium sized potatoes, boiled
2 T. lemon juice
2 medium onions, sliced very thin
Seasoning salt
2 T. chopped parsley

Slice potatoes thin and add onions and chopped parsley. Sprinkle lemon juice and seasoning salt. Toss together lightly to evenly mix the seasonings. Serve cold. *Yields: 8 servings.*

CUCUMBER AND POTATO SALAD

4 c. sliced boiled potatoes
4 c. sliced fresh cucumbers

Mix boiled potatoes and fresh cucumber, and blend with delicious **TANGY MIDDLE EAST DRESSING** (p. 35) or dressing of your choice. *Yields: 8 servings.*

CUCUMBER SALAD

4 c. sliced cucumbers   *1/2 c. thinly sliced sweet onions*
2 T. finely minced parsley

Dressing: *1 c. fresh lemon juice*
1/2 c. honey   *1/2 t. salt*

Mix salad ingredients and put into salad bowl. Pour dressing over salad. Refrigerate for a few hours stirring occasionally. *Yields: 8 servings.*

GISELE'S GREEK SALAD

1 large onion   *1 cucumber*
1 green pepper   *1/2 head cauliflower*
1–2 tomatoes   *12 olives*

Chop ingredients. Rub a large wooden salad bowl with garlic. Add all ingredients and toss. Add **GREEK SALAD DRESSING** (p. 35). *Yields: 8 servings.*

BROCCOLI GARBANZO SALAD

1 bunch broccoli
20-oz. can garbanzos, drained
1 can black olives, drained

1 recipe **TANGY MIDDLE EAST DRESSING**
Cherry tomatoes

Break broccoli into bite-sized pieces. Marinate broccoli and garbanzos in a generous amount of **TANGY MIDDLE EAST DRESSING** (p. 35). Just before serving, stir in olives. Serve on a bed of salad greens or alfalfa sprouts. Garnish with cherry tomatoes (and sprigs of fresh parsley if desired). *Yields: 8 servings.*

FRESH BROCCOLI-CAULIFLOWER SALAD

1 bunch broccoli
1 head cauliflower
1 pkg. frozen peas

1 bunch green onions
2/3 c. **GUACAMOLE DRESSING**
    mixed with 1/3 c. of water

Wash and cut or break broccoli and cauliflower in very small pieces into a large salad bowl. Clean green onions and cut into small pieces. Toss together. Add thinned **GUACAMOLE DRESSING** (p. 35). *Yields: 20 (1/2-cup) servings.*

VEGETABLE SALAD

2 c. frozen peas
1/2 c. thinly sliced celery
2/3 c. **GUACAMOLE DRESSING** mixed with 1/3 c. of water

2/3 c. finely chopped carrots
1/2 c. Spanish peanuts

Steam peas 3 minutes. Mix all. Chill. *Yields: 8 (1/2-cup) servings.*

AVOCADO SALAD

1/4 c. lemon juice
2 large avocados, cubed
4 green onions, sliced

1 small head cauliflower,
1 bunch broccoli florets

Pour lemon juice over avocado cubes and stir to coat, being careful not to bruise the cubes. Coarsely grate cauliflower and broccoli. Combine all ingredients and toss gently. Chill. Serve with soup and sandwiches. *Yields: 8 servings.*

Recipes in **BOLD PRINT** *are listed in the index.*

MACARONI SALAD

2 c. cooked w.w. macaroni	2 c. green peas
1/4 c. chopped olives	1/4 c. grated onions
1 c. shredded carrots	

The green peas may be used raw or cooked, as preferred. Mix all ingredients. Add **CASHEW MAYONNAISE** (p. 35) if desired, but delicious without dressing. Serve on a lettuce leaf. *Yields: 4 servings.*

LIMA BEAN SALAD

2 c. cooked green limas	2 c. cooked green peas
1 c. chopped celery	

Combine limas, celery and peas. Blend dressing and pour over salad. Serve immediately or chill and serve later. *Yields: 8 servings.*

MARINATED BEAN SALAD

4 c. garbanzos	
4 c. green beans	1 t. honey
1 onion, finely chopped	3 T. lemon juice

Drain garbanzos and beans and place in bowl. Add onion. [May add 1 green pepper, chopped, if desired.] Mix honey and lemon juice. Pour over beans. Salt to taste. Let stand several hours before serving. *Yields: 8 (1/2-cup) servings.*

PATCHWORK COLESLAW

1-1/2 quarts shredded cabbage
16-oz. can kidney beans, drained
1 c. chopped cucumber
1/2 c. radish slices
1/2 c. olives

Combine and toss lightly. Add **CASHEW MAYONNAISE** (p. 35) if desired, but delicious without dressing. *Yields: 6 servings.*

CABBAGE SALAD

2 c. shredded cabbage
1/2 c. grated carrot

1 c. chopped celery
1/4 c. chopped walnuts

Combine all ingredients. Add **CASHEW MAYONNAISE** (p. 35) if desired, but delicious without dressing. Serve on lettuce leaf. Garnish with pimento. *Yields: 6 servings.*

VEGETABLE PLATTER SALAD

Your choice of raw vegetables cut and arranged attractively on a large serving tray. Consider color, texture, flavor, aroma and nutrition in your choices of vegetables. Some excellent choices are carrot and celery sticks, broccoli and cauliflower florets, cherry tomatoes or tomato wedges or slices, red or green pepper rings, cucumber slices or sticks, radishes, mild onions and lettuce. Consider adding some black or green olives and one or more dips.

JERUSALEM ARTICHOKE SALAD

1 c. asparagus, cut in 1 inch slices
1 c. grated Jerusalem artichoke or
    jicama or water chestnuts

1 t. lemon juice
1/8 t. salt
1 bunch lettuce

Cook asparagus lightly and chill. Grate Jerusalem artichokes and add lemon juice and salt. Add lettuce to grated Jerusalem artichokes and toss lightly. Fold in asparagus. Top with **GUACAMOLE DRESSING** (p. 35) and garnish with 1/2 c. toasted, slivered almonds, if desired. *Yields: 4 servings.*

Salad Dressings

LIMA BEAN SALAD DRESSING

1-1/2 c. pineapple juice
2 T. lemon juice
1/4–1/2 c. cooked Lima Beans

1 t. onion powder
1 t. celery salt

Blend. *Yields: 1-1/2 cups dressing.*

Recipes in **BOLD PRINT** *are listed in the index.*

CASHEW MAYONNAISE

1-1/4 c. boiling water
3/4 c. raw cashews
1 T. honey

1 t. salt
1/4 c. lemon juice

Liquefy cashews in half of water until creamy-smooth. Still blending, add remaining ingredients, lemon juice last. **Yields:** *1 pint.*

TANGY MIDDLE EAST DRESSING

1 c. ripe green olives,
    drained and packed
1/2 c. lemon juice

1/2 c. water
1 t. salt
2 cloves fresh garlic

Liquefy all ingredients. Add herbs of your choice for taste. Ripe green olives are best. **Yields:** *1-3/4 cups.*

GREEK SALAD DRESSING

1/4 c. juice from a
    can of garbanzos

1/3 c. lemon juice
2 T. honey

Blend well. Add to salad. Sprinkle with Vege-sal (or other vegetable salt) and oregano. Let set 1/2 to 1 hour. **Yields:** *2/3-cup dressing.*

GUACAMOLE SPREAD OR DRESSING

2 ripe avocados
1 t. lemon juice
1/2 t. salt

1/3 fresh tomato
2 t. chopped onion

Blend all ingredients until smooth; or mash avocado with seasonings and finely chopped tomato and onion. Add a dash garlic salt if desired. Chill, covered. Serve fresh. Great as a salad dressing, sandwich spread, chip dip, or on vegetables. **Yields:** *2-cups dressing.*

TOMATO DIP

2 fresh tomatoes
1 T. sesame seeds

1/2 green onion, minced
1 clove garlic, minced

Whiz in blender until smooth. Dip or salad dressing. **Yields:** *6 servings.*

Fruit Salads

TROPICAL ISLE DELIGHT SALAD

2 apples
2 oranges
2 bananas

1 small can diced pineapple, drained
3/4 c. dates, chopped

Dice and toss first 3 ingredients. Add remaining ingredients. Refrigerate 2 hours before serving. Garnish with flake coconut or slivered almonds. Serve with whole wheat rolls. *Yields: 8 servings.*

FRUIT SALAD

Apples
Bananas

Blueberries or Strawberries
Sliced peaches, canned or frozen

Use enough of each kind of fruit to serve your size of family. Blend half the amount of peaches with 1 banana and a dash of honey for a sauce to be mixed into fruit.

TROPICAL HOLIDAY

1 fresh pineapple
1 ripe papaya, cubed
2 bananas

2 limes, thinly sliced
1/2 c. slivered almonds, toasted

Wash and dry pineapple. Cut in quarters lengthwise, keeping leaves intact. Remove fruit. Core and cut pineapple in chunks. Run the tines of a fork lengthwise down the peeled bananas. Slice diagonally and add to pineapple chunks. Add remaining ingredients. Carefully fill each quarter shell with the combined fruits. Pour **PINEAPPLE DRESSING** over the top. Garnish with lime slices. *Yields: 8 servings.*

PINEAPPLE DRESSING

1-1/2 c. water
1 T. honey
2 t. lemon juice

6 oz. can frozen pineapple juice
concentrate

Liquefy all ingredients until smooth. *Yields: 2-1/4 cups.*

36

E-Vegetables
Potatoes

CREAMED POTATOES

8 med. potatoes   4 c. water
1 t. salt

Cook potatoes, cool, peel, and cut into half-inch cubes. Place 3/4 of potato cubes in a mixing bowl. Put remaining 1/4 of cubes into blender and add enough hot tap water to cover 1/4 inch above potatoes. Add salt. Blend until very smooth, adding more water only if necessary keep puree moving through blender blades. Pour over potatoes and mix lightly. Place in serving bowl and serve immediately, or put into casserole to be reheated the next day at 350° F. for 20 to 30 minutes. *Yields:* 8 servings.

LAYERED POTATOES AND ONIONS

6 med. potatoes   4 c. water
1 med. onion   1 t. salt
                                   1/4 c. flour

Cook potatoes, cool and slice. Chop onion, saute in 1/4 c. water for 5 minutes. Place potatoes and onions in prepared baking dish in layers. Blend water, salt and flour until very smooth. Pour over potatoes and onions. Top with pimento cheese or bread crumbs, if desired. Bake at 350° F. until bubbly, 30 to 45 minutes. *Yields:* 8 servings.

CARROT-BROCCOLI SURPRISE

Spread cold mashed potatoes in a floured baking dish and make a depression in the center. Place 2–3 c. of cooked, seasoned broccoli and sliced carrots in depression. Cover with mashed potatoes and broil at 450° F. for 10 to 20 minutes until light brown on peaks.

Recipes in **BOLD PRINT** *are listed in the index.*

SCALLOPED POTATOES

4 c, thinly sliced potatoes
1 med. onion, sliced thin
   (or 1 t. onion powder)

1 c. cooked rice
1 to 2 c. water
1 t. salt

Prepare potatoes with or without skins and rinse thoroughly in cool water. Drain. Add sliced onion. Blend remaining ingredients until very smooth. Pour over potatoes and onions and mix thoroughly. Place in casserole dish and bake 1-1/4 to 2 hours at 375° F. Serve hot. *Yields: 6 to 8 servings.*

Note: Cover top with foil if the potatoes start to brown on top before the center is cooked. Left-over potatoes are delicious reheated in regular oven or microwave.

SLICED BAKED POTATOES

4 medium potatoes
1 t. salt

2–3 T. chopped fresh or dried herbs
(parsley, chives, thyme or sage)

Peel potatoes if the skin is tough. Otherwise just scrub. Cut potatoes into thin slices 3/4 of their depth, but not all the way through the potatoes. Lay a butter knife on cutting board on either side of the potato to prevent knife from cutting all the way through. Put potatoes in a baking dish with a small amount of water in the bottom. With fingertips, fan the slices outward to open the potatoes for seasoning and faster baking. Sprinkle with salt and herbs. Bake potatoes at 425° F. for 60 minutes until lightly browned. Check with a fork for doneness. *Yields: 4 servings.*

POTATO CROQUETTES

1 c. ground raw potatoes
1 medium onion,
   chopped fine

2 t. soy flour
1/4 c. flour
1 c. w.w. bread crumbs

Mix thoroughly; form into balls. Bake 25 minutes or until brown and crisp in 350° F. oven. Serve with gravy or favorite tomato sauce or ketchup. *Yields: 4 servings.*

Garden Vegetables

CONTINENTAL CORN

4 small to medium zucchini, quartered and sliced
2 c. kernel corn (frozen, canned, or fresh)
2 oz. jar diced pimento, drained
1/2 c. water, or less
salt to taste

Pour water into the bottom of a baking dish. Combine zucchini (leave peal on when cutting to add dark green color), corn and pimento. Toss lightly. Spoon into baking dish and heat thoroughly in 350° F. oven for 20 to 30 minutes. Serve hot. *Yields: 8 (1/2-cup) servings.*

CREOLE CORN

2 c. fresh or frozen corn
1/4 c. chopped onion
1/4 c. sliced green pepper

1 c. canned tomatoes
1/8 t. dill weed

Combine corn, onion and pepper and cook over low heat until tender. Add water if necessary. Add remaining ingredients; heat thoroughly. *Yields: 6 servings.*

KABOBS

12 very small onions
2 carrots cut into 2-inch pieces

3 med. potatoes, cut in 8 pieces
6 radishes, cut in half

Place pieces of potato, carrots, onion, and radishes on bamboo skewer sticks in alternating patterns. Place skewers in large kettle with 1/2 c. water in bottom. Steam for 20 to 30 minutes until tender. Serve with favorite vegetable or seasoned salt. *Yields: 6 servings.*

RAW VEGETABLE PLATTER

Wash and cut an assortment of your family's favorite raw veggies. Arrange nicely on a platter or large plate.

WINTER SQUASH FLUFF

3 c, cooked winter squash (Acorn, Butternut, Hubbard,
*   or any other dark yellow squash)*
1 t. salt
1/4 c. honey (more or less as needed for taste)
water

Place 3/4 to 1 c. portions of squash in blender at one time and add just enough water to allow blending action. Blend each portion 2 to 3 minutes to make it light and fluffy. In one portion add salt and honey. Mix all portions together thoroughly, and pour into a baking dish. Bake 20 minutes at 350° F. Serve hot. *Yields: 8 (1/2-cup) servings.*

CABBAGE

Chop cabbage up enough so that it will cook quickly. Put into a very small amount of boiling water, or in a water less pan with a tablespoon or so of water. Cook for only about 3 minutes.

COCONUT CABBAGE

Finely shred half a cabbage. Cook in water from one fresh coconut. Watch carefully to see that this does not burn. When crunchy, add 1/4 c. grated coconut and salt to taste. *Yields: 4 servings.*

SCALLOPED CABBAGE AND CELERY

3 c. chopped raw cabbage   *1/2 t. salt*
1/2 c. chopped celery   *1/4 c. fine bread crumbs*
1 c. Rice Cream*

Cook celery, cabbage, and salt together for 10 minutes. Turn into floured baking dish. Pour Rice Cream over vegetables. Top with crumbs. Bake for 20 minutes at 350° F. *Yields: 4 servings.*

* 2/3 c. cooked brown rice blended with 2/3 c. water.

CARROTS

When possible, scrub carrots instead of peeling them. (Sometimes the skins are bitter and should be removed.) Smaller carrots look beautiful left whole. Larger ones can be crinkle-cut or cut diagonally. Put carrots in a small amount of boiling water and cook until tender, or steam. Carrots may be flavored with sweet basil, dill weed, or a small amount of thyme or fresh chopped parsley; or try carrots in a mint sauce.

CREAMED CARROTS AND PEAS

Crinkle-cut carrots. Follow directions for **CREAMED CARROTS**, but add fresh or frozen peas for the last five minutes of cooking. Add 1 t. honey after cooking to make the peas and carrots taste younger and sweeter.

CREAMED CARROTS AND BABY ONIONS

Crinkle-cut carrots. Follow directions for **CREAMED CARROTS**, but cook baby onions with the carrots.

GREENS

Dark green leafy vegetables such as Collards, Kale, Brussel Sprouts, and Mustards are often much better if given an hour of cooking time and then thoroughly rinsed and reheated before serving. Any of the sauces listed here are good with greens. Experiment until you find your favorite.

SPROUTED LENTILS

2 c. dry lentils	1/2 t. celery salt
1 t. salt	1/2 c. onions
1-1/4 c. water	

Soak lentils 24 hours and then sprout for about 3 days. When sprouts are 1/2-inch long they are ready for use. Put last four ingredients in blender and whirl to mix and grate onion fine. Add to lentils in a kettle and cook slowly for about 20 minutes, adding more water as it is needed to make broth. Serve with Rice, Pasta, or Pizza. *Yields: 4 to 6 servings.*

Note: *Sprouts, whether from beans or grains, digest like a fresh vegetable. Thus this recipe in this section.*

F-Soups

Vegetable Soups

TAILGATE SOUP

2 quarts tomato juice
2 c. garbanzos, cooked
3 c. macaroni

1 t. dill weed
1 t. garlic salt

Bring tomato juice to a boil. Add remaining ingredients and simmer slowly until macaroni are cooked. Salt to taste. Serve hot with toast or sandwiches. *Yields: 8 servings.*
Variations: Use V-8 juice and omit seasonings. Tastes different, but is much simpler to make for travel or "tailgate" camping. Easy to make on a camp stove.

TOMATO SOUP

2 c. pureed tomatoes
4 T. water
2 T. w. w. flour

1 t. salt

2 c. cashew or soy milk, hot

Bring tomatoes to boil. Blend water, flour, and salt together as for white sauce. Add to tomatoes, and bring to boil again. Boil 3 to 5 minutes until flour thickens. Stirring constantly, slowly pour tomato mixture into cashew or soy milk. *Yields: 4 (1-cup) servings.*

TOMATO-RICE SOUP

1 quart tomato juice
1 t. salt

1 c. cooked brown rice
Onion or garlic powder to taste

Bring tomato juice to boil. Season to taste. Add cooked rice. Boil five minutes more or just until rice is heated. Pour into bowls. Garnish with a sprig of parsley if desired. Serve immediately with **SESAME OAT CRACKERS** (p. 9) or crackers or sandwiches of your choice. *Yields: 4 servings.*

*Recipes in **BOLD PRINT** are listed in the index.*

CREAM OF GARBANZO SOUP

2 c. garbanzos, freshly cooked with chopped onion
1 c. baked butternut squash   2 bay leaves

Blend garbanzos and squash and add water to get the soup consistency that you prefer. Heat with bay leaves; remove leaves before serving.
Variations: Add salt, herbs, or **Chicken-Style Seasoning** (p. 60) to taste.
Yields: 4 servings.

ASPARAGUS SOUP

1 bunch asparagus   2 t. Chicken-Style Seasoning
4 c. asparagus cooking water   2 T. arrowroot powder or
    or water   or corn starch to thicken
1/2 t. salt

Steam stalks of asparagus until tender. Whiz with remaining ingredients.
Cook until thickened. *Yields: 6 servings.*

CREAM OF CABBAGE SOUP

1 c. vegetable broth   1/2 t. salt
3 c. shredded cabbage   1 c. soy milk or cream sauce
2 T. minced onion

Cook first four ingredients for about 6 minutes. Stir in nut or soy milk. Add 2 T. minced parsley, or 1/2 t. thyme if desired. Serve with zwieback, crackers, or croutons. *Yields: 4 servings.*

FRESH GARDEN PEA SOUP

4 c. boiling water   2 t. salt
2 c. fresh peas or   1/4 small onion
    10 oz. frozen peas   1/3 c. barley or rice flour

Add peas to 1 c. boiling water. Quickly bring to a second boil and cook 1 to 2 minutes. Liquefy remaining ingredients in 3 c. water. Add partially cooked peas and water. Liquefy all ingredients, gradually adding more water if desired until mixture is creamy and smooth. Pour into pan and heat just to boiling before serving. *Yields: 6 servings.*

LIMA BEAN SOUP

2 c. lima beans
4 c. water
1 T. Chicken-Style Seasoning

1 c. frozen peas
1/2 c. soy alphabet noodles

In a smaller kettle bring first 2 ingredients to boil. Cover and simmer till done. May need to add more water while cooking. If you like, you can soak beans overnight to speed cooking time. Drain off the water and cook in fresh water. When lima beans are done blend with a little water. Add **Chicken-Style Seasoning** (p. 60) to make a cream (may add some whole lima beans). Add peas and alphabet noodles. Simmer just until peas and noodles are cooked. *Yields:* 6 servings.

HEARTY BEAN SOUP

1 lb. navy beans
1 c. onion, chopped
1 c. carrots, sliced

1/3 c. parsley, chopped
1 c. celery, chopped

Soak beans overnight. Pour off water and add enough water to cover 2-inches above beans. Bring to boil and simmer one hour, adding bay leaf and salt. Remove bay leaf. Add onions, carrots, celery, and **Chicken-Style Seasoning** (p. 60), or other savory seasonings. If you desire a thicker soup, mix 3 T. whole wheat flour with 1/4 c. water and stir until smooth, then add to soup. Heat again, stirring frequently, until thick. *Yields:* 8 servings.

Vegetable Stews

SIMPLE LENTIL STEW

1 c. lentils
3 c. water
6 thinly sliced carrots

9 new potatoes, diced
2 chopped onions
Salt to taste

Bring lentils and water to boil in saucepan. Cover and simmer until tender, approximately 35 minutes. In separate saucepan, cook potatoes, onions and carrots in a small amount of water. Serve lentils in soup bowls topped with potatoes, onions and carrots. *Yields:* 8 servings.

Recipes in **BOLD PRINT** *are listed in the index.*

SCRUMPTIOUS STEW

3 c. water with 1 t. salt
1 c. lentils
9 new potatoes, diced

2 chopped onions
6 thinly sliced carrots

Bring salted water and lentils to boil in saucepan. Cover and simmer until tender, approximately 35 minutes. In separate saucepan, cook potatoes, onions and carrots in a small amount of water. Serve lentils in soup bowls topped with potatoes, onions and carrots. Add salt to taste. *Yields: 8 servings.*

HEARTY VEGETABLE STEW

4 medium sized Irish potatoes, cubed
1 c. sliced celery with leaves
1/2 c. chopped onion, green or regular
3 c. water with 1-1/4 t. salt
3/4 c. uncooked lentils

Boil all the ingredients together in covered pot until tender. Flavor improves if stew is allowed to set for a little while before serving. *Yields: 8 servings.*

GARBANZO STEW

4 c. garbanzos, cooked or
    2 cans
1 1-lb can tomatoes
1 c. chopped onions

Salt to taste
3 T. parsley flakes

Combine and bake at 350° F. for 2 hours. Cover during last hour. (Long baking time is essential to blend flavors adequately.) Freezes well.

Fruit Soups

QUICK GOLDEN FRUIT SOUP

3 T. Minute tapioca
2-1/2 c. pineapple juice
1-1/2 c. apricot nectar

4 c. canned peaches, unsweetened
1 c. canned apricots or 1/3 c. dried

Cook tapioca in pineapple juice over low heat until tapioca is clear. Add remaining ingredients. Serve hot immediately or chill thoroughly. *Yields:* 8 *servings.*
Variations: Slice 2 bananas into it just before serving.

DEEP RED FRUIT SOUP

5 c. raspberry juice
4 T. Minute tapioca
4 c. canned pears, cubed

3 c. strawberries
2 apples, diced, with
    peelings on

Cook tapioca in raspberry-apple juice over low heat until tapioca is clear. Add remaining ingredients. Serve hot immediately or chill thoroughly. *Yields:* 8 *servings.*
Variations: Slice 2 bananas into it just before serving.

DARK FRUIT SOUP

5 c. grape juice
4 T. Minute tapioca
4 c. canned pears, cubed

3 c. blueberries
12 plums, diced, with
    peelings on

Cook tapioca in grape juice over low heat until tapioca is clear. Add remaining ingredients. Serve hot immediately or chill thoroughly. *Yields:* 8 *servings.*

G-Desserts
Ice Creams & Sherbets

PINEAPPLE SORBET

1 quart peaches canned in fruit juice
46-oz. can pineapple juice [Dole or Del Monte are best
for this Sorbet as they are higher quality and sweeter]

Whiz canned peaches and mix with pineapple juice, then freeze in your ice cream freezer for a delicious and healthful dessert. Home canned peaches are best, or purchase peaches commercially canned in fruit juice. *Yields: 8 servings.*

DATE-BANANA ICE CREAM

1-1/4 c. water   *1-2 frozen bananas*
3-5 soft dates, pitted   *2 c. frozen strawberries or other fruit*

Blend dates and water until smooth. Add bananas and fruit. Blend and serve. This should be thick as soft ice cream. *Yields: 4 servings.*

PINEAPPLE-ORANGE ICE CREAM

1/2 c. cooked brown rice   *2 ripe, frozen bananas*
1 c. orange juice   *2 oranges, peeled,*
1 c. crushed pineapple   *sectioned, frozen*
with own juice

Blend rice and orange juice until very, very smooth. Remove half of orange rice mixture from blender and add half of each of the remaining ingredients; blend until smooth. Pour into serving bowl or individual serving dishes. Repeat with remaining rice-orange mixture and other ingredients. Serve immediately as soft-serve, or return to freezer and serve within an hour. *Yields: 6 servings.*

SOY SUPREME ICE CREAM

3 c. water
1 c. Soy Supreme soy milk powder
1/2 c. honey

1 t. vanilla
1/8 t. salt

Blend all ingredients until smooth. Freeze. Put through a Champion Juicer.
Serve with Blueberry Sauce or other fruit sauce. *Yields:* *6 servings.*

HOT FUDGE SUNDAE

2 c. dates, pitted
2 c. water
3/4 c. carob

2 t. vanilla
10 large bananas, frozen
   and sliced

Heat dates in water and liquify. Add carob to make dark fudge color. Add
vanilla. Pour over frozen sliced bananas and sprinkle with nuts. Note: This
can be made by blending dates in water without heating if the dates are soft.
Try adding 1/2 c. carob and continue adding carob to taste. You may like less
than 3/4 c. carob. *Yields:* *12 servings.*

CAROB SAUCE

2 c. water
1 T. vanilla
2 T. honey

2 T. cornstarch or arrowroot powder
1/4 c. carob powder

Mix ingredients in blender, cook until starch is thickened. Good over ice
cream, sweet rolls, puddings and doughnuts. May be thickened with 1 additional T. of cornstarch or arrowroot powder and used as a spread for French
or Melba Toast. *Yields:* *2 cups.*

STRAWBERRY PINEAPPLE SHERBERT

1-1/2 c. crushed pineapple
3 bananas

3 c. frozen strawberries

Chill pineapple and bananas. Liquefy pineapple and bananas in blender.
Add strawberries a few at a time until mixture gets very thick. [Experiment
using other combinations of fruit with the bananas.] *Yields:* *8 servings.*

STRAWBERRY "ICE CREAM PIES"

Strawberry Ice Cream:

3 c. frozen strawberries
4 frozen bananas
1/2 c. orange juice or pineapple juice.

Blend half of all ingredients together at high speed until smooth. Empty blender contents into a serving bowl and repeat with second half. Return to freezer until pie crusts (below) are ready. Make pie crust. Form individual pie shells in the bottom of muffin tins. Bake. When shells are cooled, spoon ice cream into them, garnish with coconut, whole strawberries and return to freezer until serving time. ***Yields****: One 9 inch pie or eight individual (1/2 cup) pies.*

Rice Pie Crust

1 c. cashews, ground   *3/4 c. water,*
1 c. oatmeal, ground   *(more if needed)*
1 c. rice flour   *1/2 t. salt*

Combine nut meal, oats, rice flour, and salt. Mix well. Add water to form a soft dough which can be pressed into pie shell or muffin tins. Bake at 375° F. until light brown, about 10 to 15 minutes. ***Yield****: Two 9 inch" pies shells or 16 muffin cup shells.*

CAROB ICE CREAM

5 dates, pitted   *4 large ripe bananas, frozen*
3/4 c. water   *2 T. carob powder*
1-1/2 t. vanilla

Blend dates, water, and vanilla together. Remove half of liquid from blender and slowly add half of the frozen bananas, cut into 1/2-inch pieces, and half the carob powder. Pour into container and repeat with remaining half of all ingredients. Freeze or eat immediately as soft ice cream. ***Yields****: 8 (1/2-cup) servings.*

FROZEN PEACH TREATS

1/2 pound dried peaches
(soak 30 minutes in hot water)

1/2 pound pitted dates
1-1/2 c. coconut, unsweetened

Grind dried fruit together using coarse blade in food grinder. Mix with coconut. Press into 8" square pan. Sprinkle top generously with coconut and press it into the the surface. Cut in 2-inch squares. Chill to a soft frozen state. Serve. *Yields: 16 servings.*

PINEAPPLE-APRICOT FREEZE

3/4 c. dried apricots, soaked and
drained
1 c. crushed pineapple

1 mashed ripe banana
1/2 t. pure vanilla

Whiz apricots, pineapple and banana in blender. Combine all ingredients and spoon into 3 oz. paper cups. Freeze partially. Insert wooden sticks and freeze firm. Peel off paper to eat. *Yields: 6 popsicles.*

Cookies and Bars

CAROB-OAT COOKIES

1-1/2 c. quick rolled oats
3 ripe bananas
2 T. carob powder

1/3 to 1/2 c. date butter
1/2 t. salt

Whiz 1 c. of the dry rolled oats in a blender to make oat flour. Mash bananas. Combine all ingredients. Make mounds of dough on non-stick sprayed cookie sheet. Bake at 350° F. Remove from oven before they appear done. *Yields: 2 dozen cookies.*

FUDGE CAROB BROWNIES

3/4 c. honey
1-1/2 c. w.w. flour
1/2 c. carob powder

1 t. salt
2/3 c. water

Combine all ingredients except flour and stir until smooth. Add flour and mix well. Press gently into 8" square baking pan. Bake at 375° F. for 30-40 minutes. Cool; cut in 2-inch squares. *Yields: 12 bars.*

"GRANOLA BARS"

2 c. quick rolled oats	2 c. fresh or canned fruit
1/2 t. salt or to taste	1 c. dried fruit

Mix quick oats and salt in large mixing bowl. Blend fresh or canned fruit with dried fruit. Add blended fruit to oats. Mix well. Let set a few minutes for the oats to absorb liquid from the fruit. Press into a sprayed cookie sheet, 1/4 inch thick. Bake at 250° F. until chewy, 2 to 4 hours depending upon the fruit used. Score after 1 hour. If dried well, they store for a long time in the refrigerator. *Yields: 24 bars.*

PICNIC FRUIT BARS

2 recipes crisp topping	2 c. canned fruit such as
2 c. diced dried fruit such as dates,	pineapple or applesauce
apricots, prunes, pears, etc.	1/4 t. lemon extract
1 c. fruit juice.	(optional)

Simmer dried fruit with juice on low heat until dried fruit is tender. Make topping. Press half of topping into 8" square baking dish. Pour filling over topping. Pat remaining topping in place. Bake covered at 350° F. for 30 minutes, then uncover and bake for an additional 15 minutes. *Yields: 8 servings.* *Variations:* Use any of the fruit jams as filling.

PUMPKIN KHAKI BARS

1 c. rolled oats	1 t. vanilla
1 c. w. w. flour	1/2 c. honey
1/2 c. walnuts or pecans,	2 c. cooked pumpkin
finely chopped	1/2 c. water
1/4 t. salt	1/4 c. raw cashews

Combine flour and nuts; mix well and set aside. Whiz remaining ingredients in blender until smooth. Add to flour mixture and mix well. Pour into 8" x 8" baking dish and spread out smooth. Bake 20 to 30 minutes at 350° F. Cool in pan. Cut into 2 inch square bars. *Yields: 16 bars.*

Pies

LEMON PIE

2 c. pineapple juice
1/4 c. lemon juice
1/4 c. honey

3 T. grated lemon rind
1/3 c. cornstarch or Arrowroot
powder

Combine filling ingredients in saucepan and bring to boil over medium-high heat, stirring constantly. Remove from heat and pour into 10" baked pie shell. Cover the hot filling with clear plastic before cooling. Chill. Serve with sliced bananas; or sprinkle top with nuts or coconut. *Yields: 8 servings.*

CHERRY PIE

2-1/2 c. drained, pitted cherries
1 c. juice drained from cherries
3 T. quick-cooking tapioca

3 T. pure maple syrup or honey
1/8 t. almond extract (optional)

Soak tapioca in juice while making pie crust. Combine all filling ingredients. Pour into unbaked **SIMPLEST PIE CRUST** (p. 52). Bake at 375° for 40 minutes, until crust is slightly brown. *Yields: 8 servings.*

CAROB PUDDING OR PIE FILLING

1-1/3 c. water
1/4 c. carob powder
1/4 c. maple syrup

1 t. pure vanilla
2 c. cooked millet

Blend all ingredients. Pour into baked pie shell, cover with plastic, and chill. Top with **CASHEW "WHIPPED CREAM"** (p. 17) or coconut. Or pour into serving dish to serve as pudding. Chill. *Yields: 8 servings.*

SIMPLEST PIE CRUST

1 c. almond or cashew meal
1 c. brown rice or millet flour

1/8 t. salt, optional
1/4-1/2 c. water

Mix dry ingredients together in large bowl. Add water; lift-stir lightly with a fork. Press mixture into pie plate with moist fingertips. Shape edge and bake at 350° F. for 10-15 minutes. *Yields: One 10 inch crust.*

*Recipes in **BOLD PRINT** are listed in the index.*

Crisps

FAVORITE FRUIT CRISP

4 c. canned fruit (drained)	*3-1/2 T. tapioca*
1-1/3 c. juice (pineapple,	*1 T. honey (optional)*
apple, or drained juice)	*1 recipe CRISP TOPPING*

Mix fruit juice and tapioca and allow to soak 5 minutes. Combine with fruit and honey. Mix gently. Bake in baking dish, covered for 30-35 minutes, at 350° F. or until tapioca is clear. Stir once after 20 minutes. At 35 minutes, cover with topping and continue to bake uncovered until topping is golden. Experiment with different juice and fruit combinations, like apricots and pineapple juice, canned pears and grape juice. *Yields: 3–4 servings.* *Variations:* Use fresh fruit! Great with fresh apples.

CRISP TOPPING

1/4 c. pineapple juice concentrate	*1/2 t. orange rind, grated*
1/4 c. flaked coconut	*1 c. quick oats*
1/4 c. whole wheat flour	

Combine flour, orange rind and quick oats and mix well. Set aside. In either food processor or blender, Whiz pineapple juice concentrate and coconut until fine. Mix gently with fork until crumbly. Sprinkle on top of baked fruit. Bake at 350° F. for 10-20 minutes until golden. *Yields: 2 cups.*

EASY APPLE CRISP

5 unpeeled apples,	*1 c. raisins*
cored and diced	*1 c. SIMPLE GRANOLA*
1 c. unsweetened,	
crushed pineapple	

Simmer together on top of stove or bake in oven until apples are tender. Spread in a baking pan and cover with **SIMPLE GRANOLA** (p. 18) and **CASHEW CREAM** (p. 17), if desired.

Candies

CAROB CANDY

1 c. chopped dates, firmly packed
2/3 c. chopped walnuts
1-1/2 t. vanilla

2/3 c. unsweetened coconut
1-1/2 T. carob powder
Coconut for rolling balls in

Mix all ingredients together thoroughly with hands, or run through meat grinder. Form into balls 3/4 inch in diameter. Roll in coconut. Store in airtight container in refrigerator to keep from drying out. *Yields: 24 candies.*

FRUIT CHEWS

1 c. dried figs
1 c. dried apricots
1/2 c. shredded coconut

1/2 c. shredded coconut
1 c. pitted dates

Mix dried fruit and coconut. Put through a meat grinder. Shape into walnut-size balls and roll in shredded coconut. Chill. *Yields: 24 candies.*
Variations: Dried pears, raisins, prunes.

FIG SWEET-TREATS

3/4 c. dried figs
1 t. grated lemon rind

1 t. fresh lemon juice
1-1/2 c. fine coconut

Put figs through food grinder adding lemon rind and juice as it grinds. Form into 1-inch balls and roll in fine coconut. *Yields: 24 sweet-treats.*

FRUIT KISSES

2 c. mixed, ground, dried fruit
1/2 c. ground pecan meats

2 T. lemon juice

Mix and press into a roll. Wrap in plastic film. Refrigerate overnight. Slice in 1/4 inch slices with sharp knife. May be made into small balls and rolled in carob powder or unsweetened coconut. *Yields: 24 kisses.*

*Recipes in **BOLD PRINT** are listed in the index.*

Fruit Desserts

BERRIES! BERRIES!

1 c. pineapple juice
1/4 c. quick-cooking tapioca

1 t. lemon juice
4 c. blueberries or other berries

Let pineapple juice and tapioca stand in saucepan 5 minutes. Bring to a boil over medium heat. Simmer slowly, stirring often, until tapioca is clear and thickened. Add lemon juice and stir in berries. Cool. Serve as a simple chilled dessert. *Yields: 4 cups.*

FRESH FRUIT RAINBOW

1-1/2 c. pineapple or orange juice
2 T. quick-cooking tapioca
2 bananas, sliced diagonally

2 c. sliced peaches
1 c. strawberries, sliced

Soak tapioca in juice for 15 minutes. Cook over medium heat, stirring constantly, until gently boiling. Remove from heat. Allow mixture to cool, stirring occasionally. When ready to serve, fold in fruit. Decorate each serving with whole strawberries and sprigs of mint. *Yields: 8 to 12 servings.*

FRESH FRUIT SALAD DESSERT

Peel and slice several peaches
Add 1 cup of watermelon balls

Peel and slice 1 cantaloupe
Add 1 cup of blueberries

Mix 1/2 can orange juice concentrate over all. *Yields: 8 servings.*

STRUDELED APPLES

1 recipe Basic Bread dough (p. 5)
7 apples, peeled, cored,
    thinly sliced

Coriander, ground
Salt

Roll pie crust into a large rectangle. Place the apple slices on the dough covering all of the dough with a thin layer. May add raisins or chopped dates, if desired. Sprinkle apples very lightly with salt and then a generous sprinkle of coriander. Roll the strudel, beginning at one end and sprinkle dough with water if necessary to make dough stick. Seal edges. Bake at 350° F. for 45 minutes. Slice the roll like bread. Spread slices with applesauce. *Yields: 8 servings.*

H-Sandwiches

Spreads

GUACAMOLE

3 tomatoes
1/2 med. onion, diced

3 ripe avocados, quartered and pealed
1/2 t. garlic powder

Place avocados and 1 tomato in blender and whiz until smooth. Empty blended mixture into a medium-sized bowl. Cut up remaining 2 tomatoes and add them, plus the diced onion and garlic powder, to the mixture in the large bowl. Stir together. Serve as a dip. *Yields: 3 cups.*

AVOCADO SPREAD

1 fresh avocado

1/8 t. salt
sprinkle of garlic salt, optional

Peel and mash avocado. Sprinkle with salt and garlic. Crumble tofu and mix with the avocado to make a delightful cracker or sandwich spread. Also good blended as a raw vegetable dip. *Yields: About 1 cup.*

"STRING" SPREAD

1 c. cooked lentils
1-1/2 c. cooked string beans
1/2 c. pecan meal

1/2 onion, chopped
Salt to taste

Saute onions in 2 T. water. Whiz all ingredients in blender or put through meat grinder. Spoon into covered container and refrigerate to blend flavors. Serve on crackers or as a spread for bread and sandwiches. *Yields: About 2 cups.*

Recipes in **BOLD PRINT** *are listed in the index.*

GARBANZO SANDWICH SPREAD

1-1/2 c. soaked garbanzos	1 scant t. salt
2 c. water	
3/4 c. tomato paste	1 c. pitted black olives

Cook garbanzos in water and tomato paste over low heat until tender, about 1-1/2 to 2 hours. Put in blender and whiz thoroughly. Add remaining ingredients. Whiz, adding only enough water to make a thick spread. Chill well. Freezes well. *Yields: About 3 cups.*

SANDWICH SPREAD

1 can tomato puree	1 c. green pepper, chopped
1/2 c. cream of wheat cereal	1 t. onion salt
2 cans sliced olives	

Combine tomato puree, cereal, and onion salt in saucepan. Cook 5 to 10 minutes, until thickened. Add green pepper and olives. Cool. Use in sandwiches. *Yields: 16 (1/4-cup) servings.*

BEAN SPREADS

Any cooked beans (pinto, navy, kidney, garbanzo, lentils, black-eyed peas, northern, etc.) makes a tasty spread. Mash. Blend in tomato sauce or tomato puree. Season with steamed minced onion or onion powder, garlic or garlic powder, basil, parsley, celery or celery salt, olives, dill weed, paprika, etc., and a little lemon juice.

BASIC NUT BUTTER

Blend 3/4 c. nuts, adding just enough water to make desired consistency (very little for butters, more for sauces). Blend until smooth. Salt may be added. Vanilla may be added for dessert recipes. Use in place of shortening or butter in recipes.

Recipes in **BOLD PRINT** *are listed in the index.*

Burgers

VEGETABLE BURGERS

1 c. cooked oatmeal
1 raw potato, grated (include skin)
1 c. bread crumbs

1 c. walnuts or pecans,
   finely ground
2 T. onion flakes

Mix all ingredients well. Form into 6 patties. Brown on a cookie sheet in a 350° F. oven for 15 minutes. Turn and bake another 5 to 10 minutes. Serve on Burger Buns with slice of tomato, shredded lettuce or sprouts, and dressings of your choice. *Yields: 6 servings.*

LENTIL BURGERS

3 c. cooked lentils
1 c. dry w.w. bread crumbs
1 med. onion, minced

1/4 t. basil
Tomato juice

Mash lentils; cool. Add bread crumbs, onions, and seasonings. Mix in enough tomato juice to form soft dough. Form into patties. Place on cookie sheet and bake in 350° F. oven for 20 minutes. Serve in buns or in a casserole dish with tomato sauce over them. *Yields: 6 servings.*

OAT BURGERS

2 c. water
1-1/2 c. rolled oats

1/2 c. grated raw potato
1-1/2 t. onion powder
1/8 t. garlic powder

Bring water to boil; add rolled oats and lower heat. Cook 10 minutes. Remove from heat, stir in other ingredients. May add herb seasonings if desired. Shape into patties and place on non-stick cookie sheet. Bake at 400° F. for 30 minutes, until crisp around the edges. Good with tomato and sprouts on a burger bun. *Yields: 6 servings.*

QUICK-N-EASY KETCHUP

16 oz. can of tomato puree
2 T. lemon juice
1/4 t. salt

3/4 t. onion powder
1/4 t. garlic powder

Blend together or mix very well. *Yields: 2 cups.*

*Recipes in **BOLD PRINT** are listed in the index.*

Fruit Jams

DATE BUTTER

2 c. dates
2 c. water
pinch of salt

1 t. lemon juice or
other flavoring (such
as Almond extract)

Mix together and cook over medium heat until dates are cooked to mush. Add a bit more water if dates become too thick. **Yields**: *2 cups.*

PINEAPPLE-APRICOT BUTTER

3/4 c. unsweetened
pineapple juice
1/2 c. pitted dates

1/2 c. dried apricots
1/2 c. crushed pineapple
1 t. lemon juice (optional)

Soak dried fruit overnight in juice or bring to a boil in juice just before making the recipe and boil a few minutes until the fruit is softened. Blend all together. **Yields**: *2 cups.*
Variations: Replace dates with more apricots for a better color and a richer apricot flavor. Or replace apricots with peaches for **PINEAPPLE-PEACH BUTTER**.

APRICOT JAM

Simmer 1 c. dried apricots and 1-1/4 c. pitted prunes or 1 c. pitted dates in water to cover until soft. Add 1/2 c. crushed unsweetened pineapple and blend. **Yields**: *2 to 3 cups.*

RASPBERRY-GRAPE JAM

1 can frozen grape juice concentrate
1 can water
1/2 c. cornstarch
or arrowroot powder

1/8 c. lemon juice
1/4 c. honey
1 pkg. frozen raspberries

Combine all ingredients except raspberries in saucepan. Heat, stirring constantly, until thickened. Remove from heat and stir in frozen raspberries. Store in covered container in refrigerator. Keeps two weeks. Good on sandwiches, toast, waffles, French toast and over banana or soy ice cream. **Yields**: *3 cups.*

Recipes in **BOLD PRINT** *are listed in the index.*

PINA COLADA JAM

1 20-oz. can crushed pineapple
2-1/2 c. pineapple juice
1/4 c. tapioca

6. T. unsweetened coconut
1 t. vanilla (optional)

Place crushed pineapple and juice in 2 quart saucepan. Add tapioca and allow to soften for 5 minutes. Cook over medium heat, stirring regularly until
mixture is boiling and tapioca has turned clear. Add remaining ingredients.
Chill. *Yields: 3-1/2 cups jam.*

PINEAPPLE-STRAWBERRY JAM

4–5 dried pineapple rings
16-oz package fresh or frozen strawberries (or raspberries)

Place the pineapple rings on the bottom of a flat casserole dish and place the
strawberries over the rings to thaw, allowing the pineapple rings to absorb the
juice from the berries. If using frozen strawberries, soak overnight; if using
fresh berries, crush the berries to press out the juice. When the pineapple
rings have softened (4–5 hours in the strawberry juice) pour the fruit into a
blender and blend until smooth. Pour puree into a container with a lid and refrigerate. Jam will thicken as it sits. Keep refrigerated, for more than a week.
Delicious on sandwiches, toast, waffles, etc., or as a topping for banana or
soy ice creams. *Yields: 2 cups jam.*

CHICKEN-STYLE SEASONING

2 T. celery salt
2 T. onion powder
2 T. parsley flakes
2 T. turmeric

1/2 t. garlic powder
1/4 t. marjoram
1/4 c. savory

Recipes in BOLD PRINT are listed in the index. Recipes in BOLD PRINT are listed in the index. Recipes in BOLD PRINT are listed in the index. 1/4 c. salt

Mix contents and store in tightly sealed jar.

INDEX